ISBN 0 86163 024 6
©AWARD PUBLICATIONS LIMITED 1980.
SPRING HOUSE, SPRING PLACE.
LONDON NW5, ENGLAND.
REPRINTED 1981.
PRINTED IN BELGIUM.

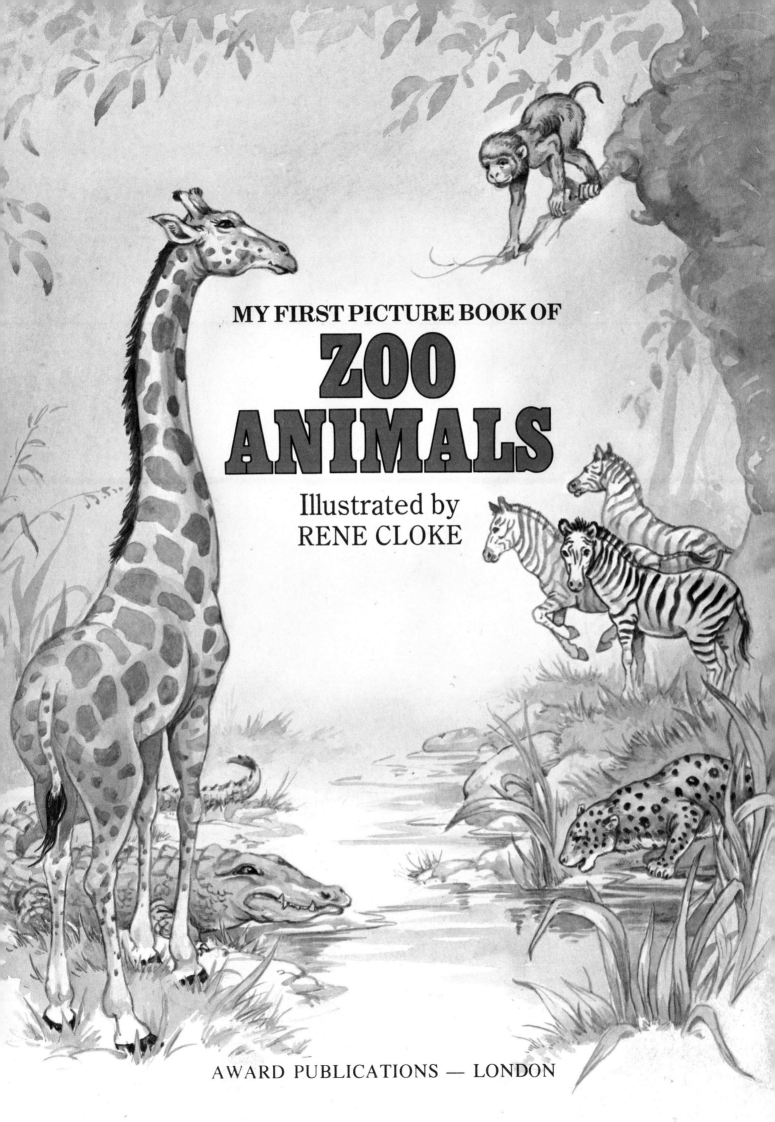

MY FIRST PICTURE BOOK OF
ZOO ANIMALS

Illustrated by
RENE CLOKE

AWARD PUBLICATIONS — LONDON

THE LION rests and sleeps a good deal in the day and hunts in the evening when smaller animals go to the waterside to drink.

The lion is patient and gentle with the cubs which are spotted when quite young; most of the hunting for the family is done by the lioness.

THE ELEPHANT

Although the elephant is the largest animal in the world, it feeds on grass, leaves and fruit.

Its trunk is very useful for gathering food and sucking up and spraying water.

Elephants like to roll in mud.

THE TIGER does not live with the family as the lion does. It is a fierce, treacherous animal and will kill even when not hungry.

Although brightly striped, it is not easily seen in the long grass of the jungle.

THE HIPPOPOTAMUS is a good
swimmer although clumsy on land.
It spends most of the day in the river and
comes ashore at night to feed on grass.

THE POLAR BEAR can walk safely on ice as its feet are covered with hair; it swims well and lives on seals.

These bears are hunted for their white furry skins.

THE GIRAFFE has a long neck which helps it to eat leaves from the trees but it has a long way to go for a drink!

THE PANDA is like a black
and white bear but is all white when born.
It feeds mostly on bamboo shoots
but will eat insects, snakes and birds when the
bamboo is covered in snow.

THE CAMEL is a rather bad-tempered animal. It can go without water for a long time and its large feet are good for walking in the desert as hoofs would sink into the sand.

Camel hair is used for making thick, warm material.

THE RHINOCEROS likes

the riverside. It is a short-sighted animal
and lives on twigs, leaves and fruit.
It will charge at its enemies with great
speed like a train and can knock over a car.

THE LEOPARD can climb trees and leap on to its prey with a lightning spring. Its spotted coat is not easily seen in the light and shade of a leafy tree.

THE MONKEY These are rhesus monkeys and they feed on leaves, fruit and grain and will also eat insects.

They are very active and spring from tree to tree in the jungle.

THE KANGAROO The mother
kangaroo carries her baby in a pouch until it is big
enough to look after itself.

The kangaroo's hind legs are very strong and
help it to leap with enormous jumps over the ground.

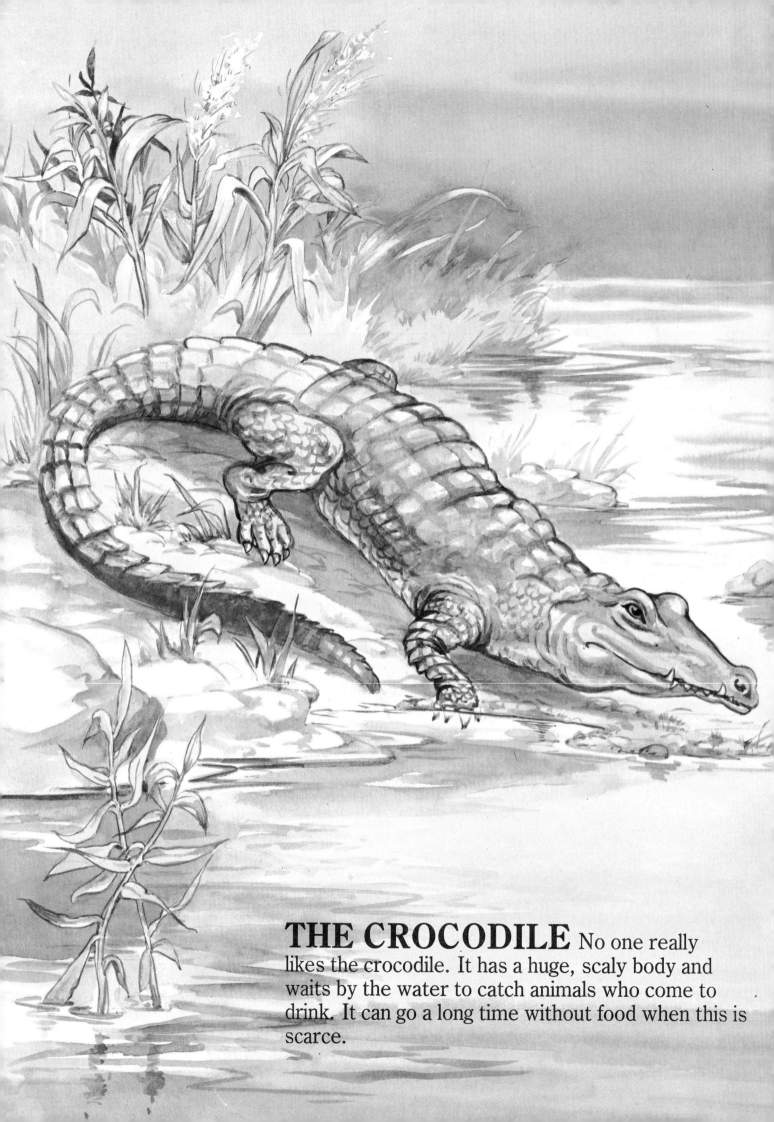

THE CROCODILE No one really likes the crocodile. It has a huge, scaly body and waits by the water to catch animals who come to drink. It can go a long time without food when this is scarce.

THE WOLF Wolves usually hunt singly or in pairs unless they are very hungry, then they gather in a pack of four or more. Those who live in a snowy country have thick woolly coats.

THE BISON live in large herds on the prairie. The herds move once a year to find fresh feeding ground.

It is not a fierce animal.

THE ZEBRA

The zebras' great enemy is the lion which attacks them when they go to the water to drink at evening.

Zebras live in herds and eat grass.